The WAKE U...

Tar...

chronicle books · san francisco

When you're feeling sleepy, try **doodling!** I bet **doodling** is fun enough to wake you up!

How does your face look when you're sleepy?

This flower is bored stiff.

Let's draw a bored dog in front of the doghouse.

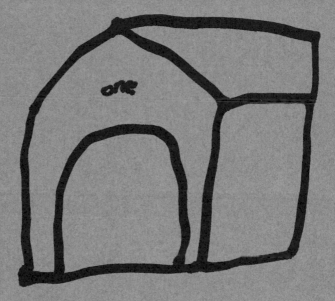

Let's draw a snoring raccoon.

**Draw some hands for
this exhausted clock.**

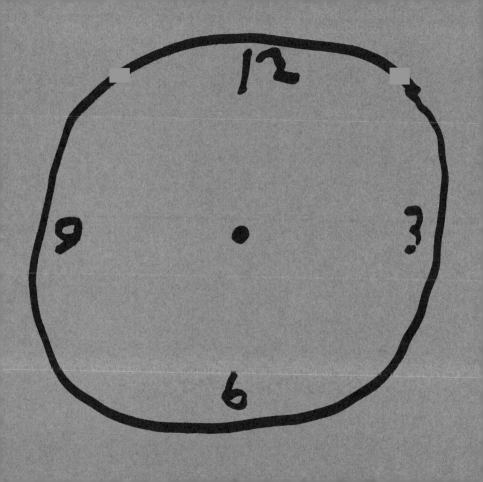

Let's draw a bored person in this house.

Let's draw some
sleepy slippers.

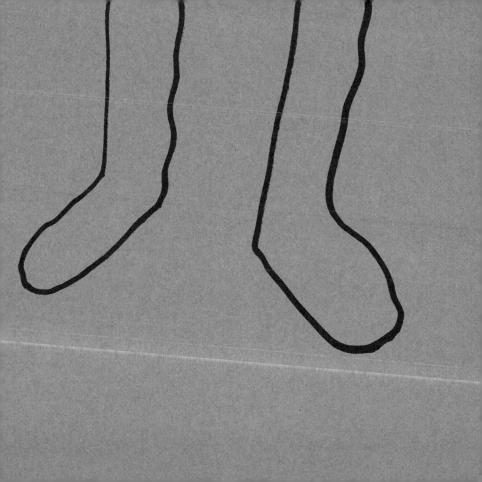

Let's draw someone riding the bike and yawning.

Let's draw a dozy person kicking the ball.

What kind of bow does she wear when she's bored?

What kind of umbrella does a sleepy person carry?

When you're feeling bored and have nothing to do, try some math!

$$\begin{array}{r} 250 \\ -\,172 \\ \hline \end{array}$$

This mountain looks
bored. Draw something
fun to make it interesting.

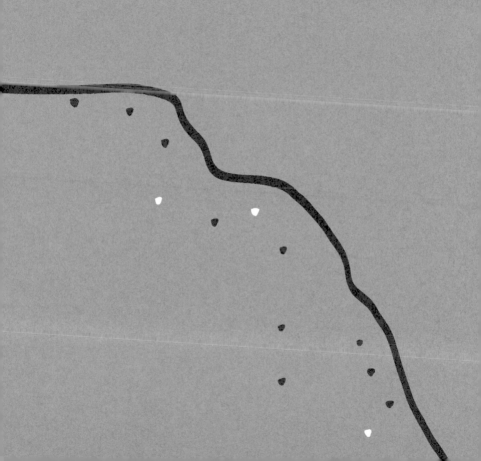

Please draw a drowsy path that continues on the next page.

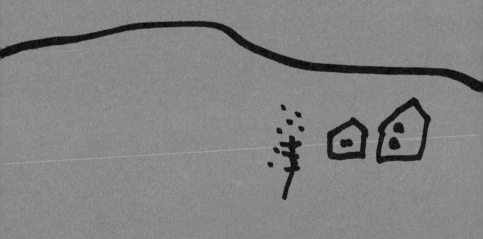

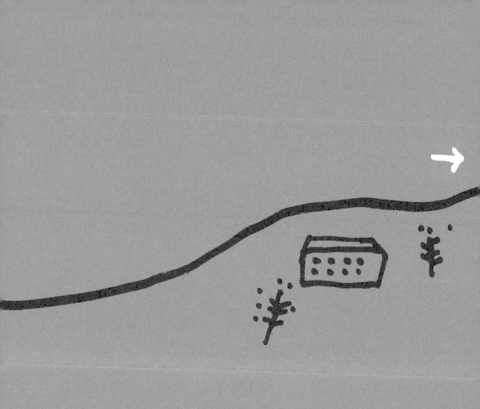

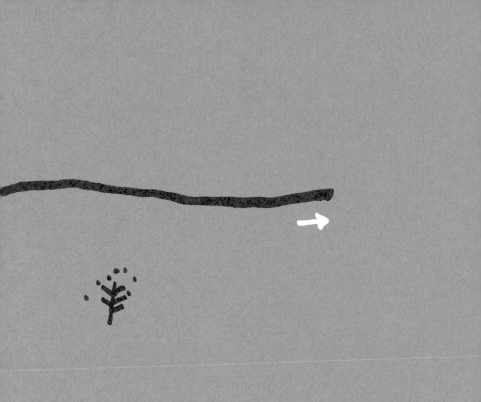

This hotel looks bored. Draw some guests to perk it up.

Let's draw someone dreaming in the bed.

Draw a yawning snowman.

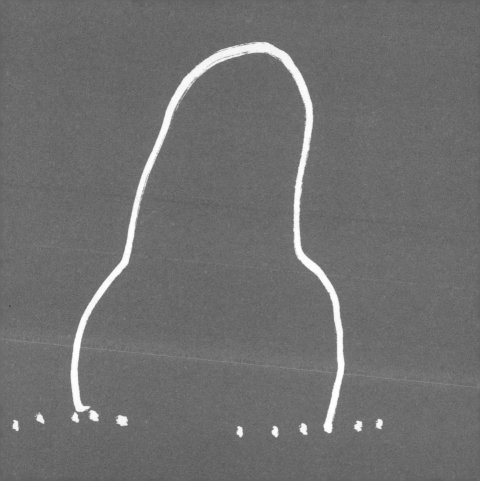

Let's absentmindedly draw
the letter **A**.

o

What kind of clothes
do you wear when
you're nodding off?

**This is a weary-looking horse.
Please make it look livelier.**

This baby is bored. Please draw some toys for her.

These cacti look very sleepy. Why don't you draw them a bird or something?

**Mom is feeling worn-out.
Please hand her something.**

How does your face look when you're wide awake? Yes, you're much more alert now. You're just fine. Now turn the page to keep doodling!

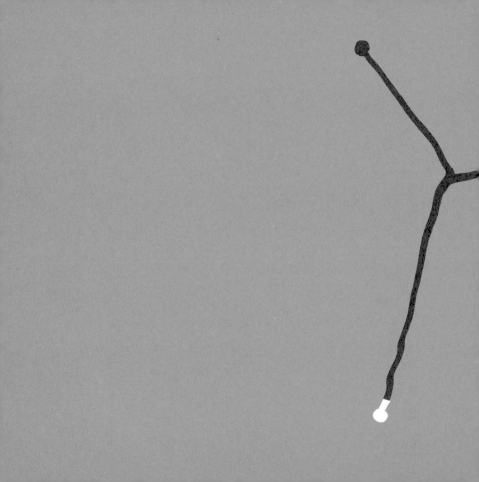

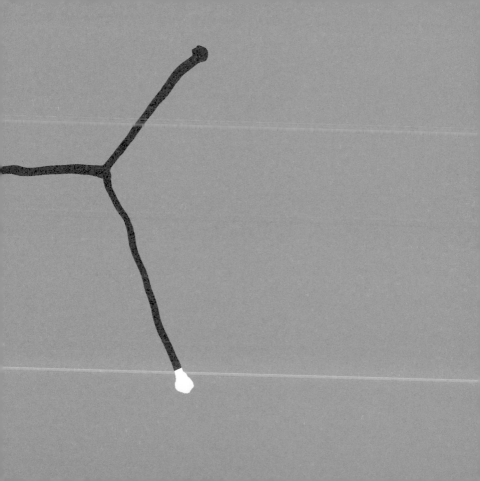

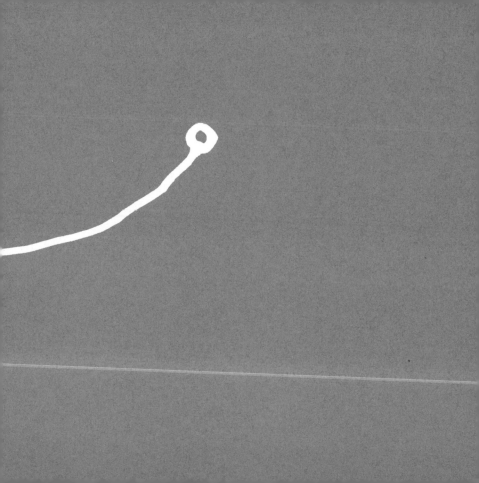

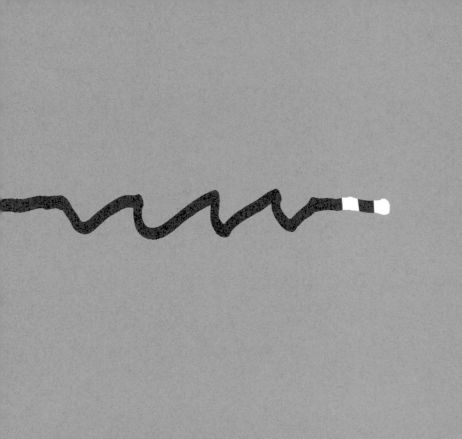

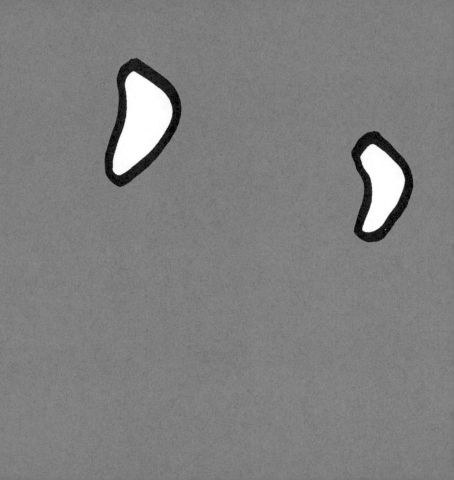

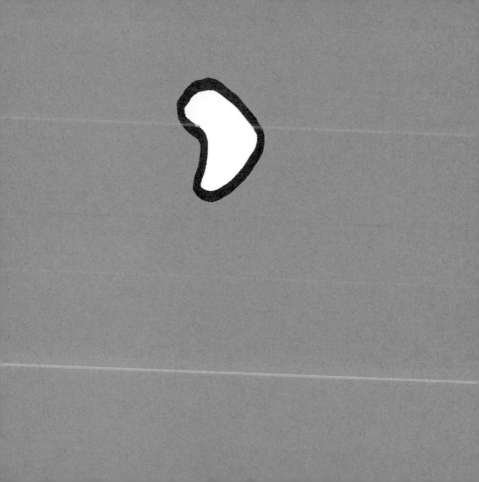

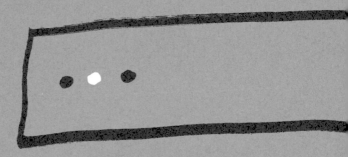

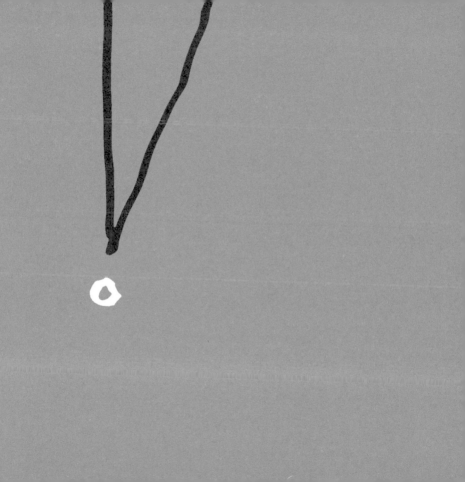

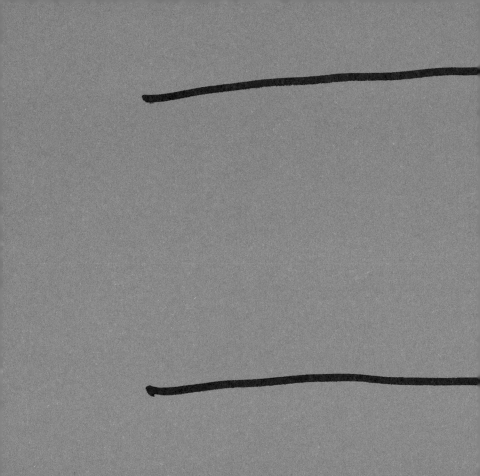

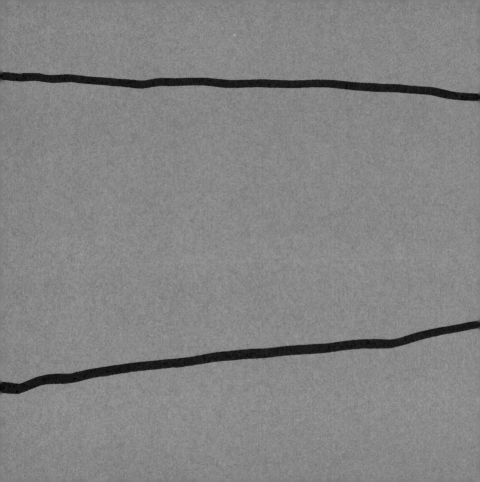

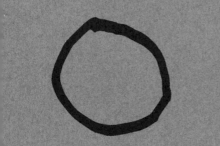
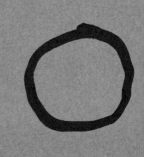

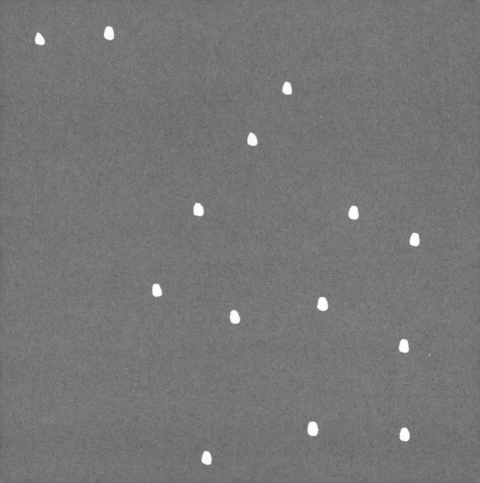

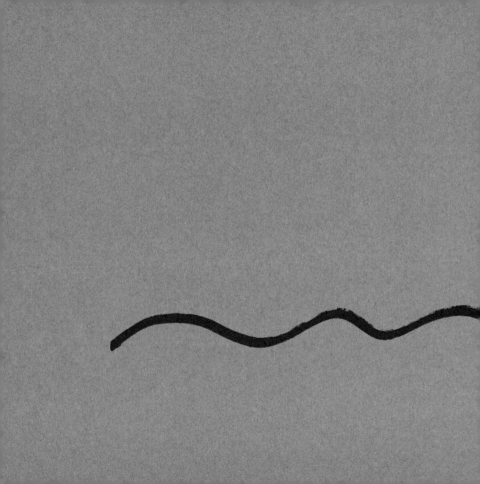

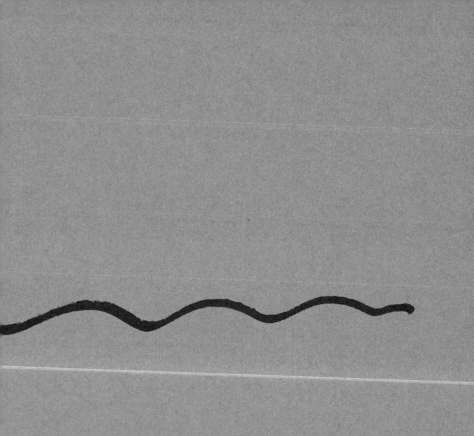

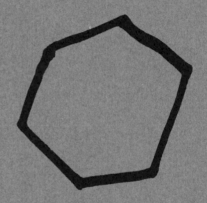

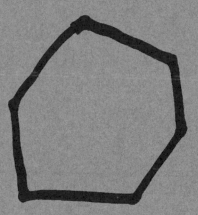

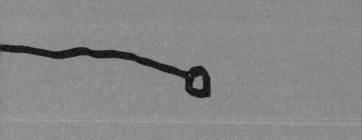

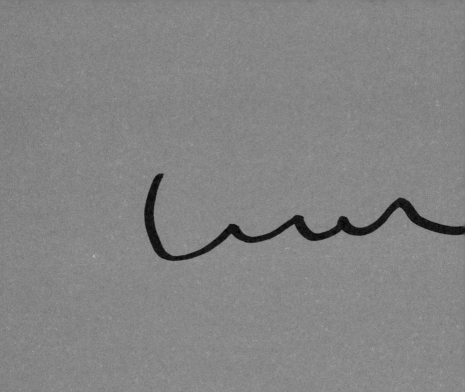

What's in the lunchbox?

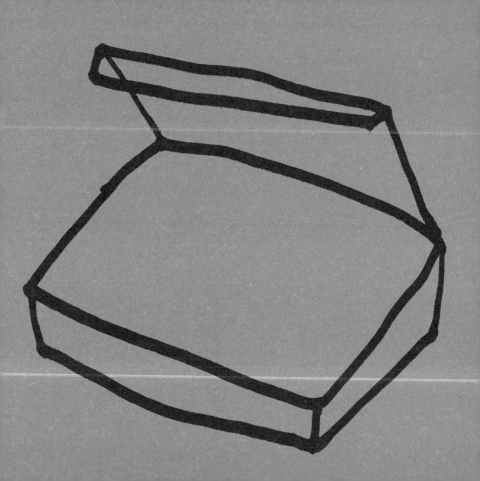

Let's draw lots of spines on the cacti.

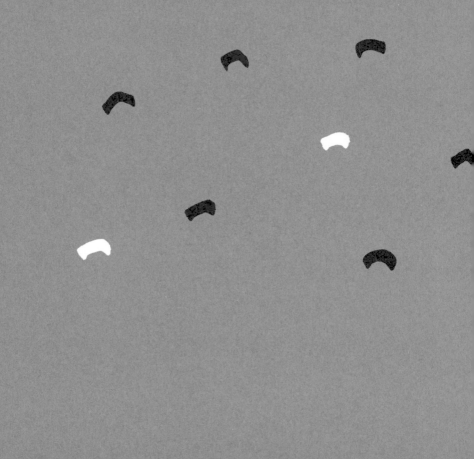

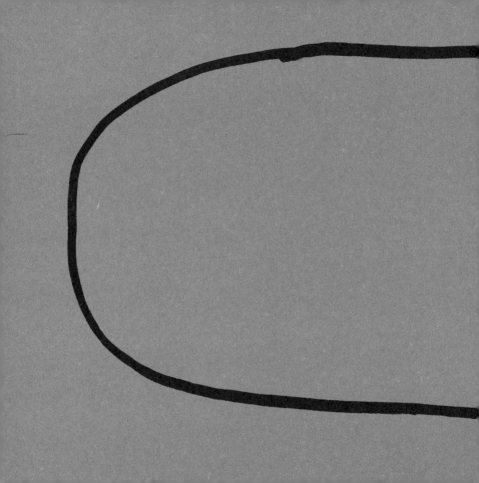

Let's write a letter to someone.

What time is it?

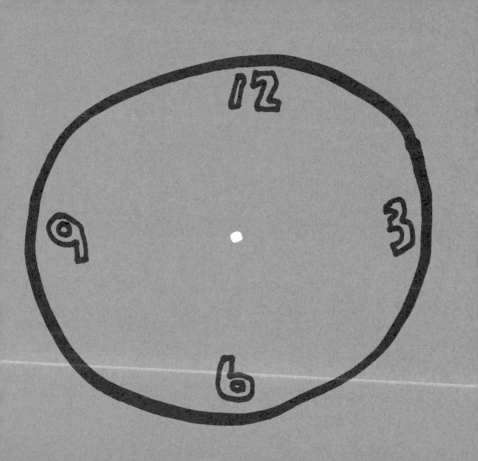

Whose underwear is this?

What do you have in your hand?

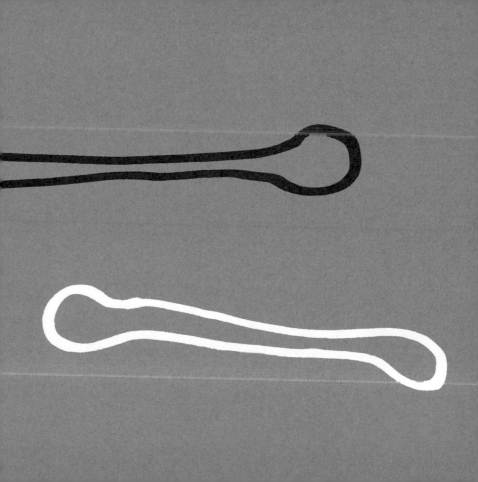

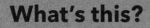

What's this?

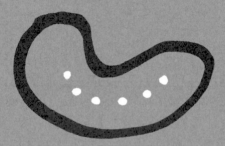

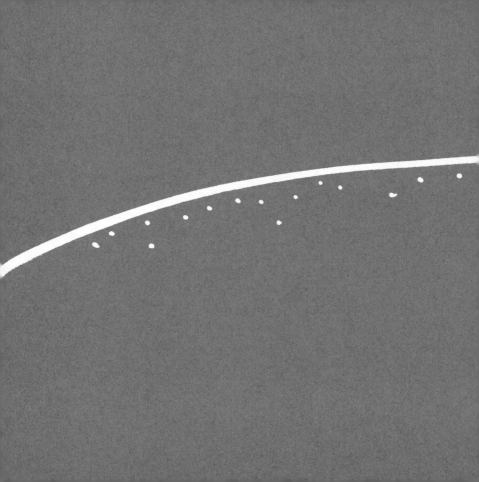

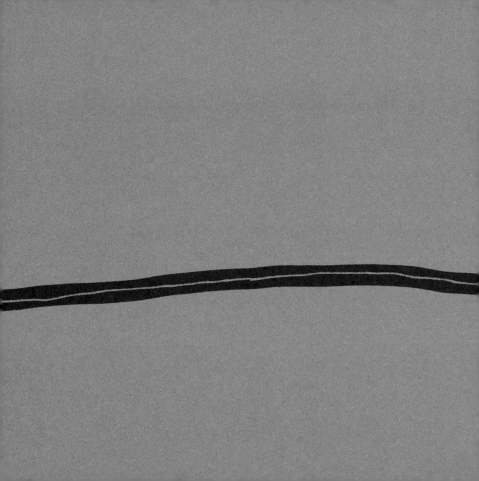

Let's draw lots of nuts.

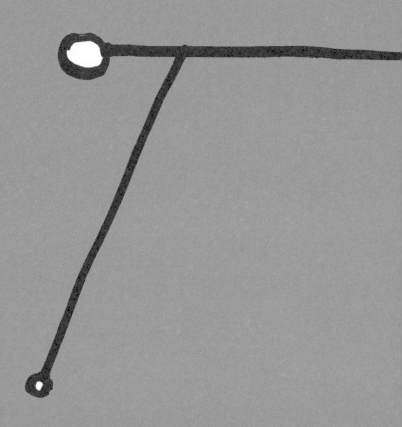

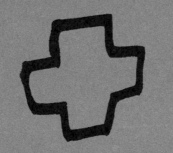

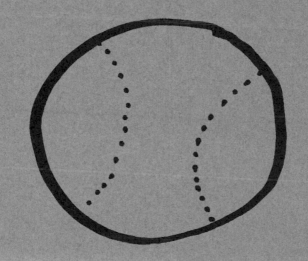

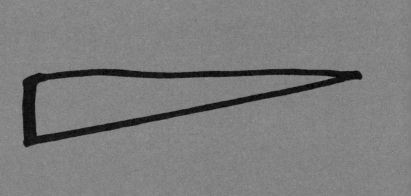

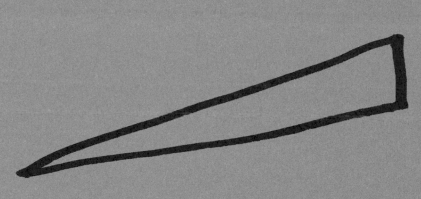

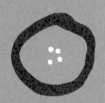

Let's draw flags.

Please draw many numbers.

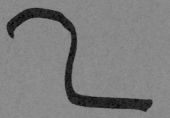

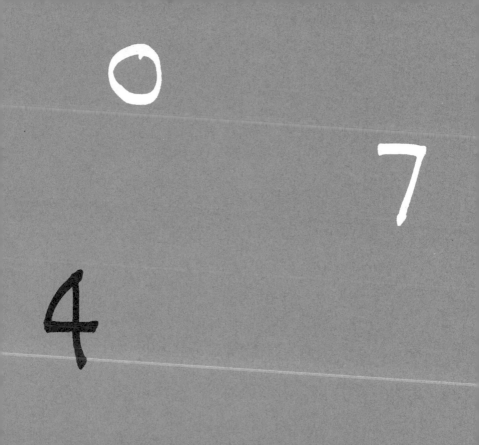

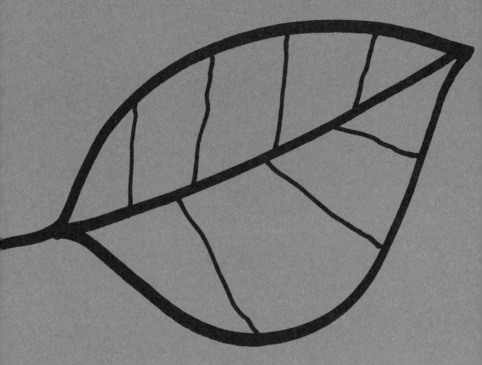

Let's draw a caterpillar.

Fill this page with lots of bugs.

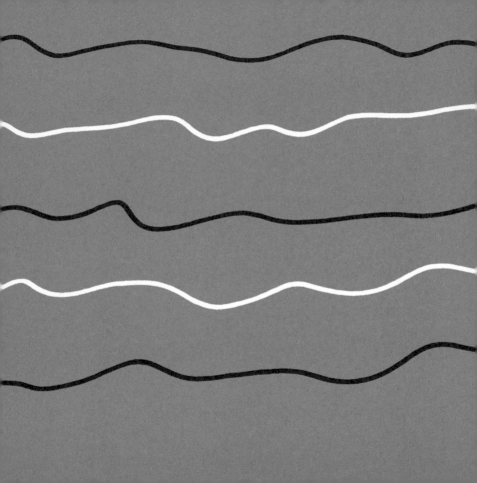

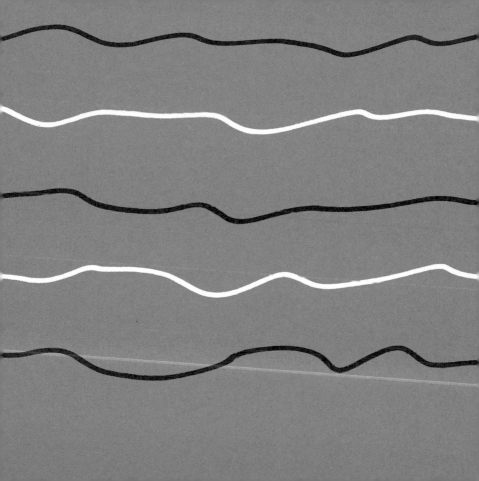

Let's hang up some clothes to dry.

What color is this elephant?

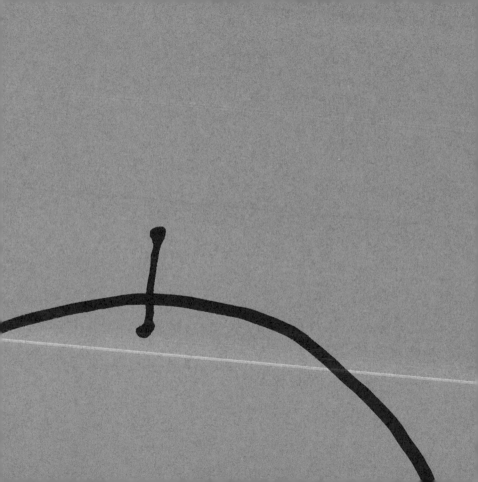

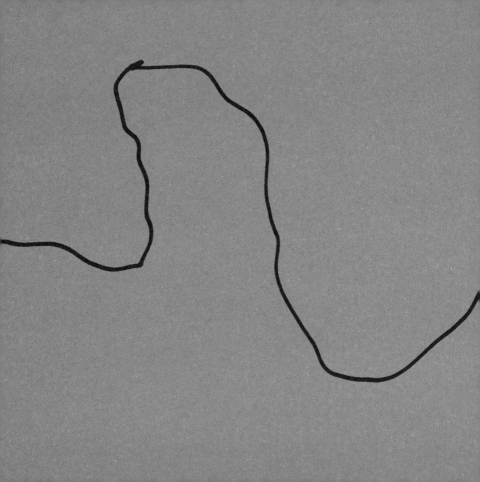

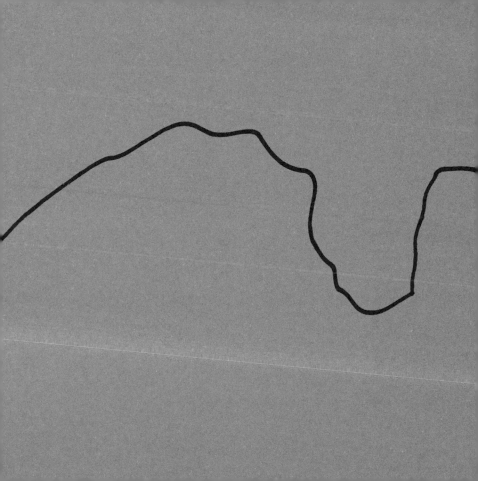

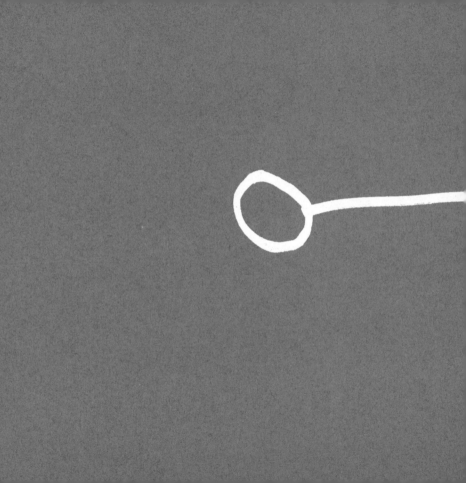

Who is sleeping in the bed?

**Knock, knock.
Someone's here.**

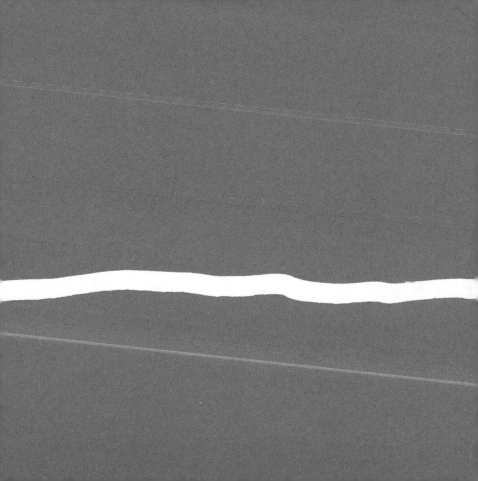

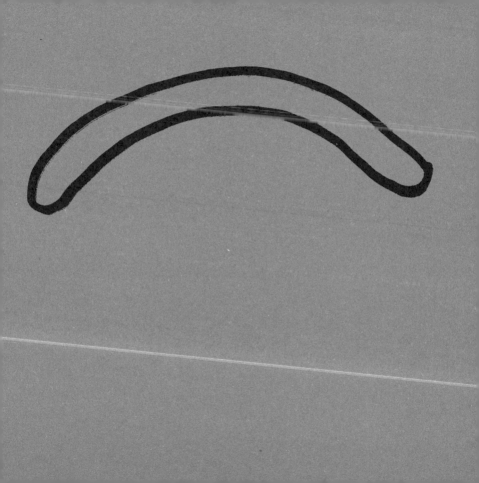

What's the feast?

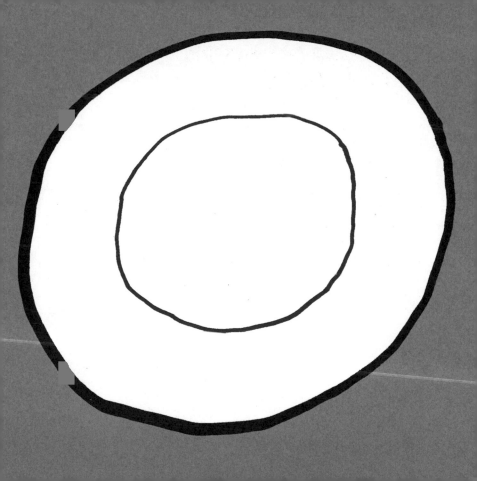

**What kind of hairstyle
will you draw?**

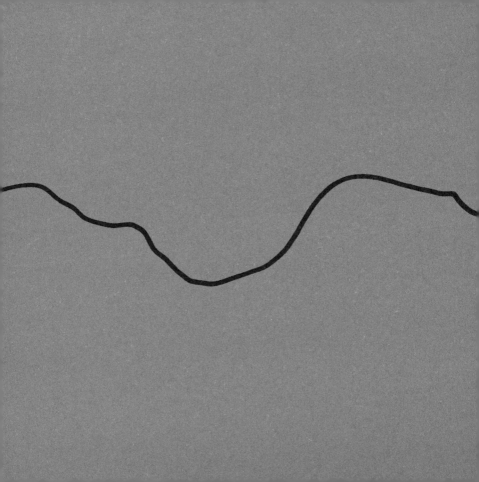

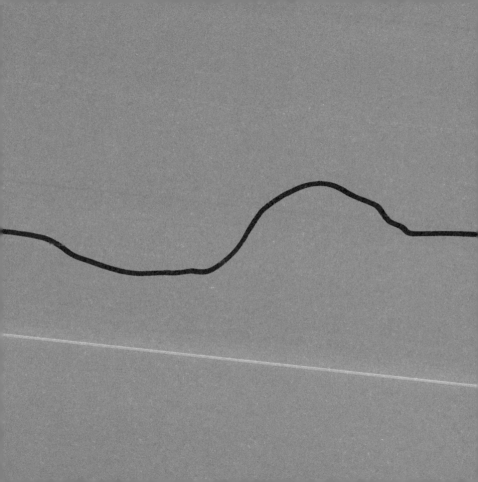

Who is in the river?

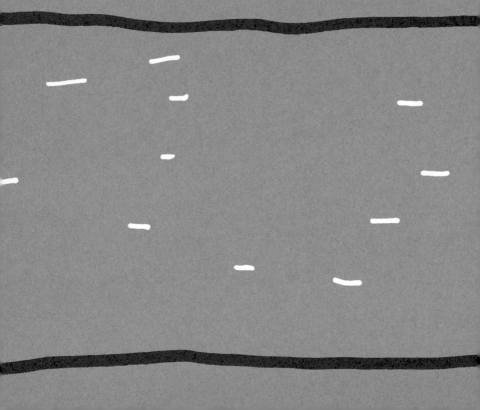

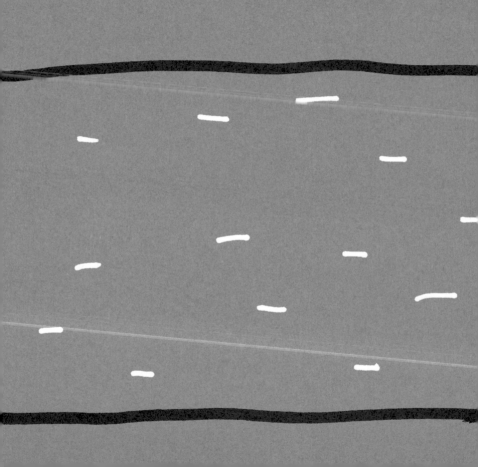

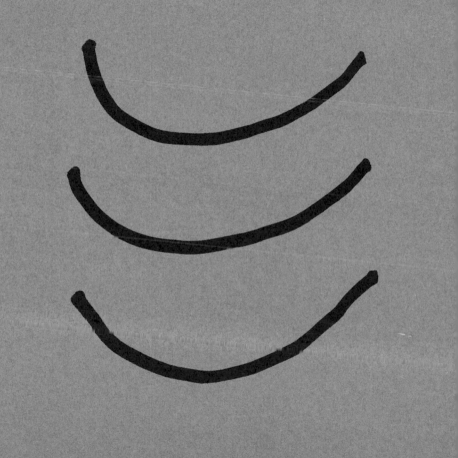

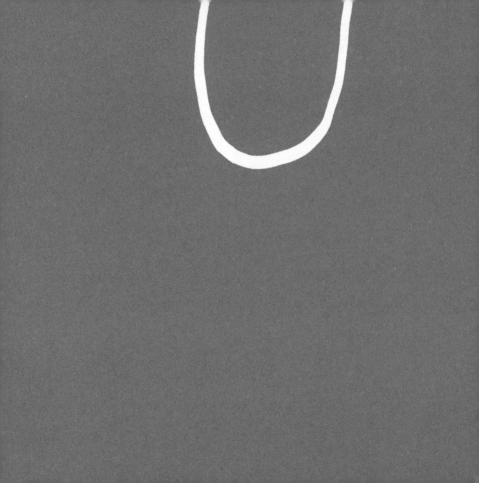

What's inside?

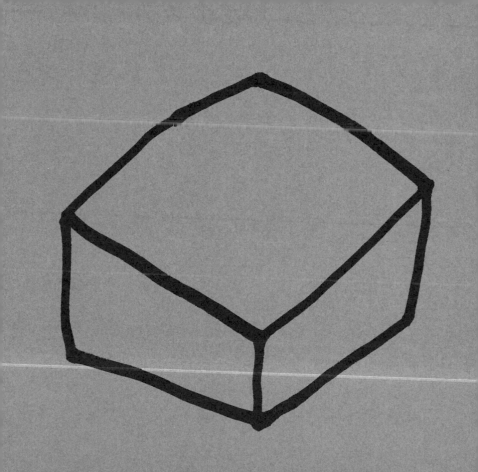

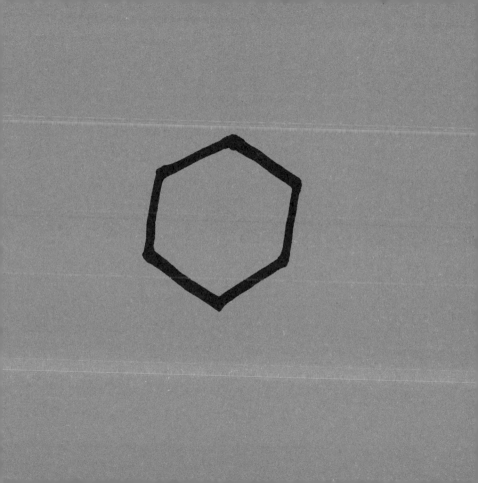

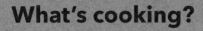
What's cooking?

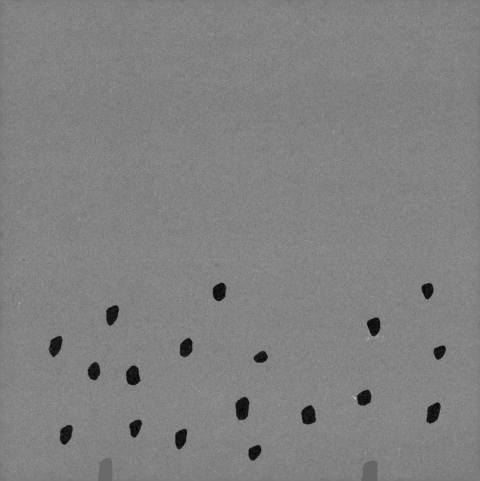

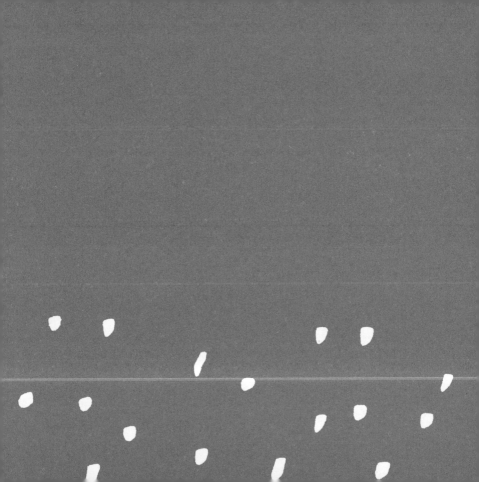

**What does this dog
have to say?**

This is the sun.

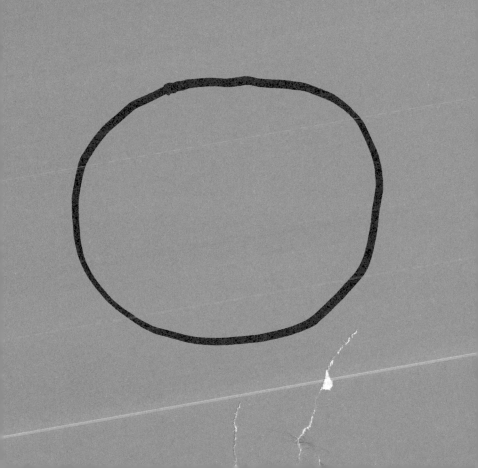

Let's go outside!